9/07

W9-BSH-583

Walkingsticks

by Emily K. Green

BLASTOFF!
READERS
2

BELLWETHER MEDIA · MINNEAPOLIS, MN

Note to Librarians, Teachers, and Parents:

Blastoff! Readers are carefully developed by literacy experts and combine standards-based content with developmentally appropriate text.

Level 1 provides the most support through repetition of high-frequency words, light text, predictable sentence patterns, and strong visual support.

Level 2 offers early readers a bit more challenge through varied simple sentences, increased text load, and less repetition of high-frequency words.

Level 3 advances early-fluent readers toward fluency through increased text and concept load, less reliance on visuals, longer sentences, and more literary language.

Whichever book is right for your reader, Blastoff! Readers are the perfect books to build confidence and encourage a love of reading that will last a lifetime!

This edition first published in 2007 by Bellwether Media.

No part of this publication may be reproduced in whole or in part without written permission of the publisher. For information regarding permission, write to Bellwether Media Inc., Attention: Permissions Department, Post Office Box 1C, Minnetonka, MN 55345-9998.

Library of Congress Cataloging-in-Publication Data
Green, Emily K., 1966–
  Walkingsticks / by Emily K. Green.
    p. cm. – (Blastoff! readers) (World of insects)
Summary: "Simple text accompanied by full-color photographs give an up-close look at walkingsticks."
  Includes bibliographical references and index.
  ISBN-10: 1-60014-015-7 (hardcover : alk. paper)
  ISBN-13: 978-1-60014-015-0 (hardcover : alk. paper)
  1. Stick insects–Juvenile literature. I. Title. II. Series. III. Series: Green, Emily K., 1966- World of insects.

  QL509.5.G73 2006
  595.7'29–dc22   2006009508

Text copyright © 2007 by Bellwether Media.
Printed in the United States of America.

Table of Contents

Walkingsticks are **insects** with long, thin bodies.

Most walkingsticks live in warm and wet parts of the world.

antennas

Walkingsticks can be many
colors. Most are green
or brown.

6

Walkingsticks have
antennas. They use their
antennas to feel and smell.

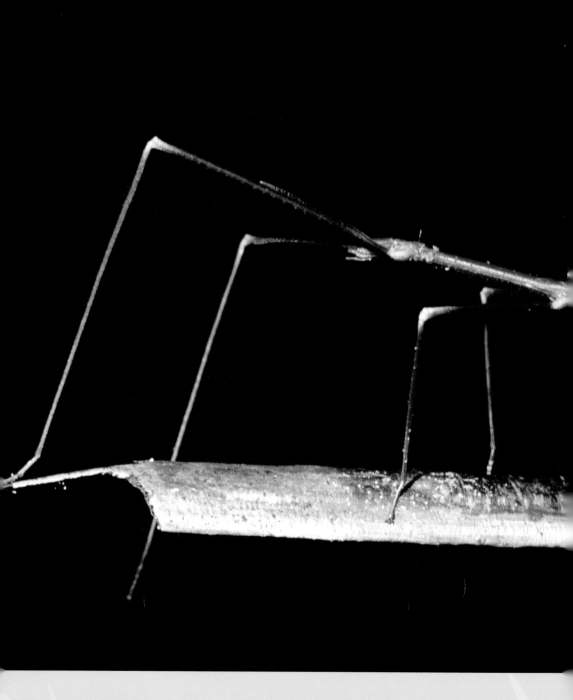

All walkingsticks have six long legs. Their front legs point forward.

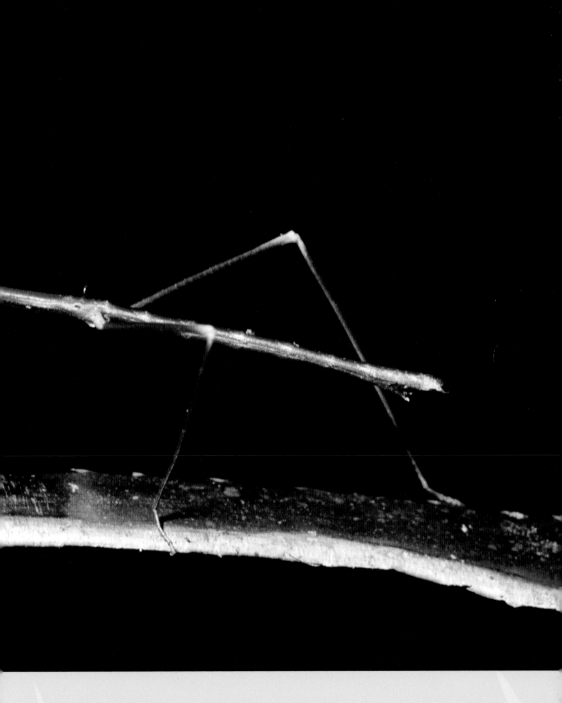

Some walkingsticks can grow
a new leg if one breaks off.

Walkingsticks have sticky
pads on their feet.

The sticky pads help walkingsticks walk upside down.

Walkingsticks know how to keep safe from **predators**.

Walkingsticks stand still during the day. They **sway** in the wind with the plants.

13

Walkingsticks move at night.

14

They move slowly while they look for plants to eat.

Walkingsticks are quiet.

Walkingsticks fall to the
ground and lie still when
there is danger.

Some walkingsticks squirt a smelly **liquid** when there is danger.

18

Some walkingsticks can change color.

They become the same color
as the plants around them.

Can you find the walkingstick?

Glossary

antennas—the long, thin feelers on an insect's head

insect—a kind of animal that has a hard body; most insects also have two antennas, six legs, and two or four wings.

liquid—something that pours like water; it is not a solid nor a gas.

predators—animals that eat other animals

sway—to move gently back and forth

To Learn More

AT THE LIBRARY

DeGezelle, Terri. *Bugs A to Z*. Mankato, Minn.: Capstone Press, 2000.

Howard, Fran. *Walkingsticks*. Mankato, Minn.: Capstone Press, 2005.

Paige, Joy. *Stick Insects: World's Longest Insect*. New York: PowerKids Press, 2002.

ON THE WEB

Learning more about walkingsticks is as easy as 1, 2, 3.

1. Go to www.factsurfer.com

2. Enter "walkingsticks" into search box.

3. Click the "Surf" button and you will see a list of related web sites.

With factsurfer.com, finding more information is just a click away.

Index

The photographs in this book are reproduced through the courtesy of: Gary Buss/Getty Images, front cover; Ra'id Khalil, pp. 4-5; Danita Delimont/Alamy, pp. 6-7, 14, 20; Nick Garbutt/Getty Images, pp. 8-9; john t. fowler/Alamy, p. 10; Rob Walls/Alamy, p. 11; Joe McDonald/Getty Images, p. 12; Jonathan Plant/Alamy, p. 13; Scott Camazine/Alamy, pp. 15, 18; Peter Arnold, Inc./Alamy, p. 16; Ian Paterson/Alamy, p. 17; Anthony Bannister/Getty Images, p. 19; Bruce Fransworth, p. 21.